PYTHON

The Ultimate Beginners Guide!

Thank you for taking the time to download this book: PYTHON, The Ultimate Beginners Guide.

This book covers the topic of python programming, and will teach you the basics.

At the completion of this book you will have a good understanding of the programming language python and be able to apply the knowledge you have learned practically.

Once again, thanks for downloading this book, I hope you find it to be helpful!

Contents

Introduction

To begin with, here a comprehension about the advancement programming dialect, Python, is provided. Python is an amazingly exceptional unique language which is easily sensible. Furthermore, it has close region with the past programming languages particularly, C, C++ and Java. This book is exceptionally useful for the novices since it has been illustrated in such a route, to the point that a learner programming designer can appreciate the phrasings used as a piece of this book. This book discusses diverse parts of python.

Firstly, it gives a brief survey of python. By then, it helps in working up the earth required for Python's setup in various working systems. Also, the central phonetic structure of Python is discussed in purpose of interest as well. This will empower the designer in making applications. Further, variable sorts and crucial executives for Python are revealed comprehensively to clear up the ambiguities. Moreover, the procedure grasped for fundamental initiative is furthermore explained in here. Despite that, loop and numbers which are used as a piece of Python are depicted here as well. Adding to this is the extraordinary capability of this book, which ensures the illustration of most of the difficulties stood up to by the novice.

These segments join strings and solace results, control stream in Python, the basic components of Python, and records and word references are furthermore elucidated in the book. In like manner, most of the edges that are basic in perception this programming vernacular are added to empower the product engineers.

Python is a straightforward yet critical dialect with such structure that underscores on the clarity. This component lessens the cost of backing of the undertaking. Python, what's more, supports packs and modules, which strengthens program measured quality and code reuse. The Python translator and the extensive standard library are accessible in source or parallel structure without charge for every single paramount stage, and can be clearly scattered.

A significant part of the time, programming engineers succumbed to Python in light of the broadened adequacy it offers. The cycle of adjust, test and investigate is extremely capable and fast as an aftereffect of the nonattendance of course of action step. Examining Python endeavors is essential: a bug or ghastly information will neglecting to bring around a division issue. On the other hand perhaps, when the referee finds a misunderstanding, it raises an exceptional case. Precisely when the undertaking doesn't get the uncommon case, the center individual prints a stack take after. A source level debugger gifts examination of nearby and general variables, assessment of subjective expressions, setting breakpoints, meandering through the code a line immediately, and so forth. The debugger is framed in Python itself, vouching for Python's contemplative force. Then again, routinely the speediest approach to manage research a structure is to add a couple print verbalizations to the source: the quick change test-investigate cycle makes this major approach unbelievably reasonable.

Chapter 1 - A Brief Overview of Python

Python is an object-arranged, integrated and a high level programming language. Moreover, its semantics is dynamic. The high level nature with data structures and dynamic typing makes python a feasible for following purposes:

i.   Connect existing components together by serving as a glue language
ii.   Efficient application development

Further, Python is an easy yet advance language with such syntax that emphasizes on the readability. This feature decreases the cost of maintenance of the program. Python, moreover, supports packages and modules, which energizes program measured quality and code reuse. The Python translator and the broad standard library are accessible in source or parallel structure without charge for every single significant stage, and can be openly dispersed.

History of Python:

Python, created by Guido van Rossum, in the late eighties and mid-nineties at the National Research Institute for Mathematics and Computer Science, in Science Park 123, 1098 XG Amsterdam, Netherlands has emerged as a big development in the programming world.

Python is derived from multiple languages which include

-   ABC
-   SmallTalk
-   Modula-3
-   Algol-68
-   C
-   C++, and
-   Unix shell

Similar to Perl, Python source code is presently accessible under the GNU General Public License (GPL). Moreover, Python is copyrighted.

Python is presently kept up by a center improvement group at the foundation, in spite of the fact that Guido van Rossum still holds a fundamental part in coordinating its encouraging.

Frequently, software engineers fell for Python in light of the expanded efficiency it offers. The cycle of edit, test and debug is quite efficient and fast because of the absence of compilation step. Troubleshooting Python projects is simple: a bug or terrible info will never bring about a division issue. Rather, when the mediator finds a mistake, it raises a special case. At the point when the project doesn't get the special case, the mediator prints a stack follow. A source level debugger permits assessment of nearby and worldwide variables, assessment of subjective expressions, setting breakpoints, venturing through the code a line at once, et cetera. The debugger is composed in Python itself, vouching for Python's contemplative force. Then again, regularly the speediest approach to troubleshoot a system is to add a couple print articulations to the source: the quick alter test-investigate cycle makes this basic approach exceptionally viable.

Python is intended to be exceedingly intelligible. It utilizes English watchwords often whereas other languages use accentuation, and it has less grammatical developments than different dialects. Following is the general overview of python:

1. **Python- An Interpreted Language:**
    Python is handled at runtime by the translator. One needs not to arrange the system before executing it. This is similar to PHP and PERL.
2. **Python- An Interactive Language:**
    It is possible to even use a Python prompt and collaborate with the mediator specifically to compose your projects. Hence, this language is quite interactive.
3. **Python- An Object-Oriented Language:**
    Python underpins Object-Oriented style or system of programming that exemplifies code inside the objects.
4. **Python- A Language for Beginners:**

Python is an amazing programming language for the fledgling level software engineers and backings the advancement of an extensive variety of utilizations from straightforward content handling to extremely important events to delights, therefore, enhancing the importance of Python.

Features of Python:

Added below are some of the most prominent features of Python:

1. **Simple in learning:**

   Python has following specialties:
   - Keywords
   - Basic structure
   - An obviously characterized syntax.

   This permits the understudy to get the language rapidly.

2. **Simple in reading:**

   Python code is all the more unmistakably characterized and noticeable to the eyes. It has been designed in such a manner that a beginner can easily understand the protocols.

3. **Simple in maintaining:**

   The source code of Python is genuinely simple to keep up. No harsh efforts are required for the maintenance of the source code.

4. **A wide standard library:**

   Python's heft of the library is extremely compact and amazingly good on the following operating systems:
   - UNIX
   - Windows, and
   - Macintosh.

5. **Intuitive Mode:**

   Python has support for an intelligent mode which permits the following:
   - Efficient testing
   - Troubleshooting of scraps of code.

6. **Convenient:**

   Python can keep running on a wide variety of equipment steps and interestingly, has the same interface on all stages.

7. **Improvable:**

   It is possible to add low-level modules in the interpreter of Python. These modules empower developers to add to or alter their instruments to be more productive.

8. **Databases:**

   Python gives interfaces to all real business databases.

9. **Graphics User Interface-GUI Programming:**

   Python support Graphics User Interface applications which therefore can be created and ported to multiple framework calls, libraries and windows frameworks, for example:

   - X Window arrangement of Unix
   - Macintosh Windows MFC
   - Macintosh

Aside from the aforementioned highlights, Python has a major rundown of good components, few are recorded underneath:

- It is versatile; Python gives a superior structure and backing for huge projects than shell scripting.
- It bolsters utilitarian and organized programming strategies and additionally OOP.
- It can be utilized for scripting. Moreover, it can be assembled to byte-code for building extensive applications.
- It provides unusual state dynamic information sorts and backings dynamic sort checking.
- It bolsters programmed junk accumulation.
- It can be effectively incorporated with the following languages:
  - C
  - C++
  - Java

- Cobra
- ActiveX
- COM

Importance of Python:

Python is vital for programming improvement. While there are all the more effective languages, quicker languages (e.g. C), more utilized languages (e.g. Java), and more irregular dialects (e.g. Haskell), Python gets many things right, and right in a blend that no other language known of has done as such far.

It perceives that you will invest significantly more energy perusing code than composing it, and spotlights on directing engineers to compose coherent code. It's conceivable to compose muddled code in Python, yet the least demanding approach to compose the code (accepting you know Python) is quite often a way that is sensible brief, and all the more essentially: code that plainly flags aim. On the off chance that you know Python, you can work with any Python with little exertion. Indeed, even libraries that include "enchantment" usefulness can be composed in splendidly lucid Python.

Python likewise recognizes that speed of improvement is imperative. Decipherable and brief code is a piece of this, as is access to intense builds that evade monotonous reiteration of code. Viability additionally ties into this - LoC might be everything except futile metric, however it says something about the amount of code you need to output, read and/or comprehend to investigate issues or change practices.

This velocity of improvement, the straightforwardness with which a software engineer of different dialects can get fundamental Python abilities, and the colossal standard library is vital to another range where Python exceeds expectations – tool making. Any undertaking of size will have assignments to computerize, and robotizing them in Python is I would say requests of extent quicker than utilizing more standard dialects - indeed, that was the way I began with Python, making an instrument to mechanize designing Rational Purify for a task where it before was such an errand, to the point that it was never run (and memory holes were not altered). I've subsequent to made instruments to concentrate data from ticket frameworks and showing them in a route valuable to the group, devices to check poms in a Maven venture, Trac incorporation, custom observing devices... furthermore, a mess more. Those devices have rushed to execute, spared a great deal of time, and a few of them has later been fixed and redesigned by individuals with no Python foundation - without breaking.

That building custom devices is simple clues at another quality - fabricating and keeping up custom programming is simple, period. This is the reason, while the very gigantic Django system may be the most renowned Python web structure, there is likewise a large group of fruitful little and miniaturized scale structures. At the point when working in a capable programming dialect with a wide cluster of standard and outsider libraries, you regularly don't have to acknowledge the exchange offs that are important when utilizing any expansive off-the-rack structure. This implies you can assemble precisely the product your clients need, as opposed to letting them know that "this is the means by which it's done, sad". To me, this is an immense contrast. I feel embarrassed when I need to tell a client that no, sad, this appears like a straightforward necessity, however the structure we utilize makes it incomprehensible or restrictively costly to actualize. At whatever point this happens, you have fizzled. Composing programming that fits into the client's model instead of into a structure is vital, and I for one feel that a ton of engineers today has dismissed that straightforward certainty. A considerable measure of software engineers now invest more energy being configurators of systems and making pardons for their deficiencies, instead of genuine programming.

Chapter 2 - Environment Setup for Python

To adequately utilize Python on the Windows operating system, one requires some sort of programming software:

- Cygwin
- Python
- Grand Text or any of the other word processor

However, use them such that each one is used in one time

Installation of Python:

- To begin with, download the desired python version from the webpage python.org.
- Now, run after opening the installer, this will install the setup to your desired location
- After this step your python is good to go

Installation of Cygwin:

Installation of Cygwin is more complicated than that of python. Follow the below mentioned steps to complete the installation:

- Download the setup from Cygwin homepage
- Now run the setup and install the software

Cygwin is a system that can be used to download as well as introduce different projects from the web for you. One need to provide it some data about the internet connection, however, more often than not you can simply acknowledge defaults and continue onward.

Afterwards, Cygwin will demonstrate to you a considerable rundown of download destinations. Every one is the very same in such a manner that you can chose one at irregular. After you've picked one and tapped the button named next now one will see an overhaul cautioning, however that lone applies to programmers redesigning from a more established adaptation of Cygwin. As it is another establishment, we can overlook it.

Presently, we get the chance to choose what programming we need to download from the website for download. We need to introduce three programming bundles:

- Openssh
- Git
- Twist.

For every one, utilize the pursuit box to discover the bundle, and after that tap on "Skip" with the goal that it manipulates to a rendition number. Introduce the most recent accessible rendition for each of all of the bundles.

Afterwards, Cygwin will let you know that you have to introduce certain different bundles as conditions. Essentially, this implies on the off chance that you need to utilize a specific bundle named X, and X depends on another bundle named Y so as to run accurately, then Cygwin might distinguish this and request that introduce bundle Y too. You can simply hit "Next". By then, Cygwin will begin downloading and introducing all the bundles that one has asked for, and in addition every one of their conditions. Contingent upon the velocity of your web association, this might take some short period of time. At the point when the center among all the three advancement bars is full. Now, Cygwin is done.

On the off chance that you request that Cygwin introduce a symbol on your computer, and then this will do as such, making an alternate way known as Cygwin Terminal. You will utilize this symbol to run your Python code, and additionally to get to the following:

- Openssh
- git, as well as
- Twist bundles that you introduced.

Moreover, double tap the symbol to open the Cygwin program. This will open a Cygwin window. To advise Cygwin about how to connect with Python, run the below mentioned command:

"PATH=\$PATH:/cygdrive/c/Python32" >> .bash_profile

Note that you are utilizing the registry that you introduced Python into; in case you're introducing an alternate variant of Python, and then supplant Python32 with the rendition of Python you have introduced. You ought to just have to do this one time: later you've run that order; the program will dependably have the capacity to discover Python once more. This marks the completion of Cygwin installation.

Installation of text editor:

In the end, you will require a text editor. Although, numerous great alternatives can be used but , Sublime Text is suggested because of following qualities:

- It is effective and helpful
- It has boundless free trial.

Moreover, it must be noted that Microsoft Word is not used as text editor but as a word. Therefore, you cannot utilize Microsoft Word for programming purposes.

In order to install Sublime Text, follow the steps stated below:

- Browse to Sublime Text webpage
- Secondly, download the required setup
- Run and install the setup

Further, it is not among one of the software which is free; however, a trial can be conducted for an unlimited time. Yet it is recommended to buy the license.

After installation, now run a program to testify the working of everything. A beginner in programming language usually starts any language by writing "This is the beginning" in a programming language.

$ python -c 'print("This is the beginning")'

This is the beginning

After this, open the Sublime Text and write following in it:

#!/usr/bin/env python

print("This is the beginning")

Afterwards, save this file on the home directory i.e., your C directory as beginning.py

Now open your command prompt and write following command and stimulate.

$ chmod a+x beginning.py

$ ./beginning.py

This is the beginning

The display of similar output verifies the successful installation of your software. Here you are good to go and start your journey of Python learning.

Chapter 3 - Basic Syntax for Python

Python is a broadly utilized high-level, universally useful, deciphered, dynamic programming dialect. Its outline theory underscores code comprehensibility, and its punctuation permits software engineers to express ideas in less lines of code than conceivable in dialects, for example, C++ or Java. The dialect gives develops expected to empower clear projects on both a little and substantial scale.

Python underpins various programming standards, including object-arranged, basic and practical programming or procedural styles. It includes a dynamic sort system and modified memory organization and has an expansive and far reaching standard library.

Python mediators are accessible for some working frameworks, permitting Python code to keep running on a wide assortment of frameworks. Utilizing outsider devices, for example, Py2exe or Pyinstaller, Python code can be bundled into stand-alone executable projects for the absolute most prominent working frameworks, so Python-based programming can be disseminated to, and utilized on, those situations with no compelling reason to introduce a Python translator.

CPython, the reference usage of Python, is free and open-source programming and has a group based advancement model, as do about the greater part of its variation executions. CPython is overseen by the non-benefit Python Software Foundation.

Python is a user friendly language which can be understood easily by the beginners. Some of the things to be noted during the first program are as follows:

- It must be noted that all python records will have augmentation .py. During working on the first program, the programmer must observe the file extension to avoid any errors during compilation.
- The above stated advice can be explained by following example:
- Print "Hello, World"; in a file named check.py

- Now, in order to run this program use the command i.e., $ python test.py
- The result of this will be Hello, World

1. Identification/Naming:

i. Moreover, in Python you must identify or name the following things carefully and accurately
- Variable
- Function
- Class
- Module
- Object

ii. During naming, you must observe that an identifier always starts with an English alphabet A to Z, a to z or even an underscore. This can be followed by any number, ranging from 0 up to any number.

iii. One of the greatest approaches of learning programming demands that the programmer must discover about the errors that arise if protocols are not followed.

iv. Python does not allow accentuation characters for instance, ^, #, (and inside identifiers.

v. Python is a case delicate programming language

vi. Subsequently, Paris and paris are two diverse identifiers in Python.

vii. It is in the syntax of Python that a class name always starts with one of the uppercase letters. Whereas other identifiers starts with a lower case letter

viii. By convention, any identifier starting with a single leading underscore depicts that the identifier is supposed to be private.

ix. Moreover, an identifier with double underscore depicts that the identifier is extremely private.

x. Further, if any identifier has two underscores which are trailing then this means that the name of identifier is a special name defined by the language.

2. Keywords:

Some of the words which are reserved keywords in Python are as follows:

- and
- assert
- from
- print
- finally
- exec
- not
- or
- break
- for
- pass
- class
- continue
- global
- raise
- def
- if
- return
- del
- import
- try
- elif
- in
- while
- else
- is
- with
- except
- lambda
- yield

3. Indentation and lines:

- In Python, no braces are required to demonstrate the following
    - i.   Chunk of code for class
    - ii. Functions definitions
    - iii. Flow control
- Blocks of code are indicated by line indentation, which is strongly imposed.
- The quantity of spaces is variable in the indentation, yet all of the statements inside the block must be indented by the same sum.

Correct indentation

```
if True:
    print "True"
 else:
    print "False"
```

Incorrect indentation

```
if True:
    print "Answer"
print "True"
else:
    print "Answer"
print "False"
```

Attempt a couple of various cases to get hands on with Python.

4. Multiple lines statement:

- Consider the following code with multiple lines:
- Numbers = Number_one + \

- Number_two + \

- Number_three

- However, note that the statements contained inside the following do not require the use of line continuation character

    i. []
    ii. {}
    iii. ()

- For instance:
- WeekDays = ['Monday', 'Tuesday', 'Wednesday', 'Thursday', 'Friday']

5. Quotations:

- Python acknowledges single ('), twofold (") and triple ("' or""") quotes to mean string literals the length of the same kind of quote begins and finishes the string.
- The triple quotes can be utilized to traverse the string over numerous lines. e.g.
- word = 'word'
- sentence = "This is a sentence."
- paragraph = """This is a paragraph. It ismade up of multiple lines and sentences. """

6. Comments:

- All characters after the # and up to the physical line end are a piece of the comment and the Python translator overlooks them.
- For example:
- # this is a comment
- print "Hello, Python!";
- # this is another comment and the compiler will ignore it
- Whereas, in order to comment multiple lines, follow the following method, by using these signs you will ignore the text written in between. The greater part of the lines underneath are ignored by the translator

- """ One can add multiple lines in between. These are all comments. Thus ignored by the compiler """

7. Wait for the user:
- The accompanying line of the program depicts the following prompt:
- "Press the enter button if you want to exit" and holds up for the client to press the Enter key:
- raw_input("\n\nPress the enter button if you want to exit.")
- Moreover, here, these signs i.e., "\n\n" are being utilized to make two new lines before showing the genuine line.
- Once the client presses the key, the project closes.
- This is a decent trap to keep a console window open until the client is finished with an application.

8. Several statements on single line:
- Here we use semicolon (;) which permits numerous announcements on the single line given that neither statement begins a fresh code piece.
- Here is an example which depicts how to utilize the semicolon:
- import sys; y = 'foo';
- The same as
- import sys;
- x =
- 'foo';

9. Suites
- A group of several statements, which make a single code square are known as the suites in Python.
- Compound or complex proclamations, for example, if, def, while, and class, are those which require a header line and a suite.

- Header lines start the statement with one of the keyword and end with a colon (:) and are trailed by one or more lines which make up the suite.

For example:

if expression :

suite

elif expression :

suite

else :

suite

Chapter 4 - Variable Types and Basic operators for Python

To start with, operators are all those structures which can control the estimation of operands. Consider the expression 2*4=8. Here, 2 and 4 are called operands and * is called the operator.

Variables:

In programming, a variable or scalar is a capacity area combined with a related typical name (an identifier), which contains some known or obscure amount of data alluded to as a worth. The variable name is the typical approach to reference the put away esteem; this division of name and substance permits the name to be utilized autonomously of the accurate data it speaks to. The identifier in PC source code can be bound to a worth amid run time, and the estimation of the variable may accordingly change over the span of project execution.

Variables in programming may not straightforwardly compare to the idea of variables in science. The estimation of a registering variable is not as a matter of course part of a condition or recipe as in science. In registering, a variable might be utilized in a redundant procedure — doled out a quality in one spot, then utilized somewhere else, then reassigned another worth and utilized again as a part of the same way (see cycle). Variables in PC writing computer programs are as often as possible given long names to make them generally graphic of their utilization, though variables in science regularly have brisk, maybe a couple character names for quickness in interpretation and control.

A variable stockpiling area might be eluded by a few unique identifiers, a circumstance known as associating. Appointing a worth to the variable utilizing one of the identifiers will change the quality that can be gotten to through alternate identifiers.

Compilers need to supplant variables' typical names with the real areas of the information. While a variable's name, sort, and area regularly stay settled, the information put away in the area might be changed amid system execution.

The center of this part is an inside and out take a gander at each of the ways that we can assess code, and compose significant squares of contingent rationale. We'll cover the points of interest of numerous administrators that can be utilized as a part of Python expressions. This part will likewise cover a few subjects that have as of now been talked about in more significant detail, for example, the circling develops, and some essential project stream.

Operators:

We'll start by talking about subtle elements of expressions. In the event that you'll recollect from Chapter 1, an expression is a bit of code that assesses to deliver a worth. We have seen a few expressions being used while perusing through the past parts. In this part, we'll concentrate more on the internals of administrators used to make expressions, furthermore distinctive sorts of expressions that we can utilize. This section will really expound on how we can characterize pieces of code for circling and conditionals.

This part will likewise expound on how you compose and assess numerical expressions, and Boolean expressions. What's more, to wrap things up, we'll talk about how you can utilize enlarged task operations to consolidate two or more operations into one.

Types of Expressions

An expression in Python is a bit of code that delivers an outcome or worth. Regularly, we consider expressions that are utilized to perform numerical operations inside our code. Nonetheless, there are a large number of expressions utilized for different purposes too. In Chapter 2, we secured the subtle elements of String control, succession and word reference operations, and touched after working with sets. The majority of the operations performed on these articles are types of expressions in Python. Different case of expressions could be bits of code that call strategies or capacities, furthermore working with records utilizing cutting and indexing.

All of those operators which Python supports are given below:

- Logical Operators
- Membership Operators
- Assignment Operators
- Identity Operators
- Comparison Operators
- Arithmetic Operators
- Bitwise Operators

Moreover, these operators are explained in the coming text.

1. **Logical operators:**

   The logical operators which are supported by Python language are elaborated in the coming examples. Begin this by considering a has a value of 20 and b is 5.

   - **Logical "AND" :**

     This case refers to situation when both of the operands are true, then consequently the condition becomes true. For example:

     (a AND b) in this case is true.

   - **Logical "OR" or "or":**

     In this case when one of the operands is true i.e. non-zero, then consequently the condition becomes true. For example:

     (a OR b) in this case is true.

   - **Logical "NOT" or "not":**

     NOT is used to reverse the state of the operand. For example:

     NOT(a and b) is false in this case

2. Membership operator:

The membership operator of Python tests for the membership in a succession, for example, lists, tuples or strings. Following are the two membership operators along with examples:

- **"in":**

    This operator checks and turns true if it finds the desired variable in the required series or sequence. However, it turns false if the desired variable is not in the required sequence. For example: a in x, here the outcome of in is a 1 if a is a member of the sequence x.

- **"not in":**

    This operator checks and turns true if it does not find the desired variable in the required series or sequence. However, it turns false if the desired variable is there in the required sequence. For example: a not in x, here the outcome of not in is a 1 if a is not a member of the sequence x.

3. Assignment operator:

In order to understand assignment operator, consider two variables x and y, such that x is equal to 10 and y is equal to 20. Now each assignment operator is explained below separately:

- **"="**

    This operand assigns values from the right side operands to the operand of left side. For example,

    z = x + y assigns the value of x + y into z. Here z becomes equal to 30.

- **"+= Add AND"**

    This operator adds the right operand to the operand on the left side. Moreover, it assigns the result to left operand. For example:

    z += x is equivalent to z = z + x

- **"-= Subtract AND"**

    This operator has a duty to subtract the right operand to the operand on the left side. Moreover, it assigns the result to left operand. For example:

z -= x is equivalent to z = z − x

- **"*= Multiply AND"**

  This operator multiplies the right operand to the operand on the left side. Moreover, it assigns the result to left operand. For example:

  z *= x is equivalent to z = z * x

- **"/= Divide AND"**

  This operator divides the right operand to the operand on the left side. Moreover, it assigns the result to left operand. For example:

  z /= x is equivalent to z = z /x

- **"%= Modulus AND"**

  This operator takes modulus of the two operands. Moreover, it assigns the result to left operand. For example:

  z %= x is equivalent to z = z %x

- **"**= Exponent AND"**

  This operator is responsible in performing exponential calculation on the operators. Moreover, it assigns value to the left operand. For example:

  z **= x is equivalent to z = z ** x

- **"//= Floor Division"**

  This operator is responsible in performing floor division on the operators. Moreover, it assigns value to the left operand. For example:

  z //= x is equivalent to z = z // x

4. **Identity operators:**

   Identity operators are used to compare the memory locations of any two objects. Following are two Identity operators elaborated below:

   - **"is"**

     This operator is used to evaluate if the variables on either side of the operator point to the same object, and false in the other case. For example:

     a is b, here the outcome is 1 if id(a) are id(b) are equal.

   - **"is not"**

This operator is used to evaluate if the variables on either side of the operator point to the same object, and true in the other case. For example:

a is not b, here the outcome is 1 if id(a) are id(b) are not equal.

5. **Comparison operator:**

These operators are used to compare the values on both sides. Moreover, they decide the relation among them. Further, they are also known as relational operator. In order to understand them, consider x= 10 and y= 20;

- **"=="**

  This condition becomes true when the values of two variables are equal. Here in this case (x==y) is not true.

- **"!="**

  This condition becomes true when the values of two variables are not equal.

- **"<>"**

  This condition becomes true when the values of two variables are not equal. Moreover, this operator has resemblance with! = operator. Here (a <> b) is true.

- **">"**

  This condition becomes true when the value of left variable is greater than the value of right variable. Here (x > y) is not true.

- **"<"**

  This condition becomes true when the value of left variables is less as compared to that of the right one. Here (x <y) is true

- **">="**

  This condition becomes true when the values of left variables is greater than or equal to than that of the right one. Here (x >=y) is not true

- **"<="**

  This condition becomes true when the values of left variables is less than or equal to than that of the right one. Here (x <=y) is true

6. Bitwise operator:

This operator does bit wise operations. First the number is converted into binary then the respective operations are performed accordingly.

Following are some of the bitwise operators:

- AND
- OR
- XOR
- Compliments
- Binary shifts

7. Arithmetic operators:

These include the following operators:

- Addition
- Subtraction
- Multiplication
- Division
- Modulus
- Exponent
- Floor division

Chapter 5 - Decision making in Python

In python, decision making is foresight of conditions happening while execution of the system and determining moves made by conditions. Choice structures assess various expressions which create TRUE or FALSE as result. You have to figure out which move to make and which articulations to execute if result is TRUE or FALSE generally.

The capacity to settle on choices based off of information is a standout amongst the most fundamental parts of programming. Python, as most dialects, does this by means of the "if" or comparable explanations.

The flow chart given below is one of the typical algorithms for decision making found in the greater part of the programming dialects:

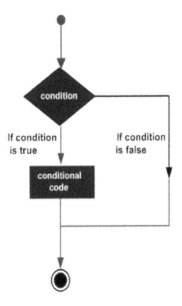

Decision making is required when we need to execute a code just if a specific condition is fulfilled. In this programming language, it assumes any non-zero and non-null values as TRUE. However, if it is either a zero or null it is assumed as

FALSE value. Following are some of the decision making statements that are used in Python:

1. **"if" statements:**

   Any if statement in Python comprises of a Boolean expression which is followed by some other statements.

2. **"if..else" statements:**

   Interestingly, the "if" statement can be nested by any else statement. This, in return, runs when the stated Boolean expression is FALSE.

3. **Nested if statements:**

   You can utilize one if or else if nested in another if or else if statement.

Chapter 6 - Loops and numbers in Python

Loops:

In programming, loop is a grouping of directions that are constantly reiterated until a specific condition is achieved. Normally, a specific procedure is done, for example, getting a thing of information and evolving it, and after that some condition is checked, for example, whether a counter has achieved an endorsed number. In the event that it hasn't, the following guideline in the arrangement is a direction to come back to the primary direction in the succession and rehash the grouping. In the event that the condition has been achieved, the following guideline "fails to work out" to the following successive direction or branches outside the loop. Moreover, a loop is considered to be a major programming thought that is generally utilized as a part of composing projects.

An unending loop is one that does not have a working way out routine. The outcome is that the loop rehashes ceaselessly until the working framework detects it and ends the project with a mistake or until some other occasion happens

Generally, statements are executed successively: The main statement of the function is executed initially, trailed by the second and this sequence keeps on going. A situation might come when you have to execute a square of code a few number of times. Therefore, most of the programming languages give different control structures that work for multiple paths and cycles which are complicated. Following flow chart depicts the working of a loop

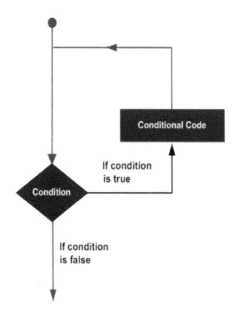

This programming language gives the following kinds of loops to handle the cycling requirements.

1. **While loop:**

   This loop keeps on repeating the statement or group of statements till the provided condition is TRUE. This, consequently, tests the condition before the loop body is executed.

2. **For loop:**

   This statement is responsible to execute a sequence of statements several times and shortens the code which thus controls the loop variable.

3. **Nested loops:**

   One can employ one or multiple loop inside any while, for or do..while loop.

Loop control statements are responsible to change execution from the typical arrangement. At the point when execution leaves an extension, all programmed objects that were made in that degree are crushed. Python bolsters the accompanying regulating statements:

- Break statements:

  Ends the loop and exchanges execution to the statements instantly taking after the loop body.

- Continue statements:

  This is responsible for the loop to avoid the rest of its body and promptly retest its condition preceding reiteration.

- Pass statement:

  The pass statements used in Python are utilized whenever an announcement is required however you don't need any order or code to execute.

Numbers:

Numbers are those types that store numeric qualities. They are unchanging information sorts, implies that changing the estimation of a number information sort results in a recently distributed item. Objects of numbers are established when a person assign certain value to these objects. For example

- Num1 = 1
- Num2 = 10

There is also another opportunity to delete the reference to a number object. For this use the del statement. Thus, to achieve this you have to follow the syntax of the del statement. The syntax is as follows:

- del Num1[,Num2[,Num3[....,NumN]]]]

One can also delete single or several objects by using the del statement. For example:

- del Num
- del Num1, Num2

Python underpins four distinctive numerical sorts:

- **int (marked whole numbers):**
  They are regularly called just whole numbers or ints, are certain or negative entire numbers with no decimal point.
- **Long numbers :**
  Also known as longs, they are whole numbers of infinite size, composed like whole numbers and took after by a capitalized or lowercase L.
- **float :**
  They depict reak numbers and are composed with a decimal point partitioning the whole number and fractional portion. these floating numbers may likewise be in experimental documentation, with E or e demonstrating the power i.e., raised to that of of 10
- **Complex numbers :**
  These are of the structure x + yJ, where x and y are floating numbers and J (or j) speaks to the square base of - 1 (which does not exist). The real portion of this number is x, and the nonexistent part is y. Complex numbers are not utilized commonly in Python.

Python changes over numbers inside in an expression containing blended sorts to a typical sort for assessment. Be that as it may, now and then, you have to force a number unequivocally starting with one write then onto the next to fulfill the prerequisites of any operator or even the parameters of functions.

- Write int(a) to change over a to a plain whole number.
- Write long(a) to change over a to a long whole number.
- Write float(a) to change over a to a coasting point number.
- Write complex(a) to change over a to a mind boggling number with genuine part a and fanciful section zero.

Write complex(a, b) to change over a and b to a number which is complex who has a as a real part and y as the imaginary part. However, a and b are numeric expressions

Chapter 07- Strings and console output in Python

A string is typically such content one need to depict. Python knows you need something to be a string when you put either " two-quotes or " single-quotes around the content. You saw this on multiple occasions with your utilization of print when you put the content you need to go inside the string inside "or "after the print to print the string.

Strings may contain the arrangement characters you have found in this way. You just put the designed variables in the string, and after that a % (percent) character, trailed by the variable. The main catch is that on the off chance that you need different organizations in your string to print various variables, you have to put them inside ( ) (bracket) isolated by , (commas). It's as though you were instructing me to purchase you a rundown of things from the store and you said, "This is a string".

Strings are amongst the most prominent sorts in Python. We can make them basically by encasing characters in quotes. Python regards single quotes the same as twofold quotes. Making strings is as basic as appointing a quality to a variable.

Accessing values in strings:

Python does not bolster a character sort; these are dealt with as strings of length one, along these lines likewise considered a substring. To get to substrings, utilize the square sections for cutting alongside the record or files to acquire your substring.

str1 = 'Hello World'

str2 = "This is a string"

print "str1[0]: ", str1[0]

print "str2 [1:5]: ", str2[1:5]

Updating strings:

You can redesign a current string by (re)assigning a variable to a string. The new esteem can be identified with its past worth or to a totally distinctive string through and through.

str1 = 'Hello World!'

print "Updated String : ", str1[:6] + 'Python'

Console output:

Console output is a profitable apparatus for issue analysis. It is particularly valuable for investigating bit issues and administration setup issues that could bring about an example to end or get to be inaccessible before its SSH daemon can be begun. Thus, the capacity to reboot examples that are generally inaccessible is profitable for both investigating and general occurrence administration.

EC2 occurrences don't have a physical screen through which you can see their console yield. They likewise need physical controls that permit you to control up, reboot, or close them down. Rather, you play out these undertakings through the Amazon EC2 API and the order line interface (CLI).

Generally as you can reset a PC by squeezing the reset catch, you can reset EC2 cases utilizing the Amazon EC2 console, CLI, or API. For more data, see Reboot Your Instance.

Caution:

- For Windows examples, this operation plays out a hard reboot that may bring about information defilement.

Example Console Output:

For Linux/Unix examples, the occasion console yield shows the accurate console yield that would typically be shown on a physical screen joined to a PC. This yield is cushioned in light of the fact that the occasion produces it and after that presents it on a store where the example's proprietor can recover it.

For Windows occasions, the case console yield shows the last three framework occasion log blunders. The posted yield is not constantly overhauled; just when it is prone to be of the most esteem. This incorporates not long after example boot, after reboot, and when the occurrence ends.

To get console yield utilizing the console

- Open the Amazon EC2 console
- In the left route sheet, pick Instances, and select the occurrence.
- Pick Actions, Instance Settings, Get System Log.
- To get console yield utilizing the order line
- You can utilize one of the accompanying orders. For more data about these order line interfaces, see Accessing Amazon EC2. get-console-yield (AWS CLI) ec2-get-console-yield (Amazon EC2 CLI)

For more data about regular framework log blunders, see Troubleshooting System Log Errors for Linux-Based Instances.

Catch a Screenshot of an Unreachable Instance

In the event that you can't achieve your example by means of SSH or RDP, you can catch a screenshot of your occasion and view it as a picture. This gives ability to precieve with regards to the status of the example, and takes into account snappier investigating.

To get to the occasion console, following the steps shown below:

- Open the Amazon EC2 console.
- In the left route sheet, pick Instances.
- Select the example to catch.
- Pick Actions, Instance Settings.
- Pick Get Instance Screenshot.

Occurrence Recovery When a Host Computer Fails

In the event that there is an unrecoverable issue with the equipment of a fundamental host PC, AWS may plan an occasion stop occasion. You'll be told of such an occasion early by email.

To recoup an Amazon EBS-upheld case running on a host PC that fizzled

- Move down any vital information on your case store volumes to Amazon EBS or Amazon S3.
- Stop the example.
- Begin the example.
- Reestablish any imperative information.
- [EC2-Classic] If the example had a related Elastic IP address, you should reassociate it with the occasion.

To recoup a case store-upheld example running on a host PC that fizzled

- Make an AMI from the example.
- Transfer the picture to Amazon S3.
- Move down imperative information to Amazon EBS or Amazon S3.
- End the example.
- Dispatch another case from the AMI.
- Reestablish any essential information to the new example.
- [EC2-Classic] If the first occasion had a related Elastic IP address, you should relate it with the new example.

Chapter 08 - Control Flow in Python

A project's control flow is the request in which the system's code executes. The control stream of a Python project is managed by contingent proclamations, cycles, and calling of function. This segment covers the if explanation and for keeping in mind cycles; capacities are secured later in this part. Raising and taking care of special cases likewise influences control stream

It is vital to control the system execution in light of the fact that in genuine situations the circumstances are loaded with conditions and in the event that you need your undertaking to duplicate this present reality closer then you have to change those true circumstances into your system. For this you have to control the execution of your project proclamations. This article is about controlling the system execution succession. It is ordinarily known as control stream in programming terms. So we should make a plunge the stream of system explanations that is controlled by python control stream apparatuses.

The main word is control that basically implies controlling. We don't need the default conduct, we need diverse one. We are getting the diverse conduct by controlling a few parts of the conduct. Presently it comes to flow; Flow is only a way or succession of system execution. As a matter of course every announcement of system is executed one by one according to the pattern in which they show up in a project code. When we consolidate the above two words we get control flow, that basically implies controlling the stream of system execution to get want conduct or result. Utilizing control stream we are controlling the announcement execution, now program will never again be executing in succession, the execution is controlled by control devices. To comprehend it we should take couple of case, in a bank administration program we would prefer not to allow the recuperate ability to work if the trade out a record is zero. In that case we have to skirt the recovery program code and that is control stream.

Tools to control flow in python:

Python give different apparatuses to stream control. Some of them are as follows: if , if .. elif .. else, if..else, else,for, while ,pass, switch, range, break, proceed with, capacity and so forth.

-    If – else if:

This control proclamation show that if something happens then do this. It's a decent method for taking care of some short conditions. Moreover, if piece can be trailed by zero or any number of else square then the answer will be false.

-    For statement:

It is utilized for cycling over a succession. Python doesn't bolster old for loop or loop for c language. In conventional style for circle we have one variable which repeats over a grouping and we can change the estimation of arrangement and variable also yet in present day for loop we have emphasis variable that emphasizes over a settled succession. We cannot change the arrangement and in addition emphasis variable amid repetition.

-    Break:

Break is utilized for ending the cycle strangely i.e. that even the grouping is not finished but rather circle is left. The break articulation is permitted just inside the body of loop. At the point when break executes, the ending of loop. On the off chance that a cycle is settled inside different iterations, break ends just the deepest settled loops. In viable utilize, a break explanation is for the most part inside some proviso of an if proclamation on top of it body so it executes restrictively.

-    Continue:

Continue is utilized for proceeding to next cycle of the loop but without doing anything inside the respective loop.

- Else:

Else is presented in python and it is set in loop but without if. It will execute only if the loop is ended without any break.

- Pass statement:

Pass proclamation is utilized when you would prefer not to do anything other than it is required because it is syntactically correct. Pass has two basic employments.

- It is utilized for making insignificant classes.

- It is utilized as spot holder. For instance consider the accompanying scrap

Therefore, the most ideal approach to do that is to simply hone what we have realized. In the event that you need, you can make a project for printing the prime numbers somewhere around 1 and 100. On the off chance that one has finished that program then that implies you comprehend the stream control.

Chapter 09-Functions in Python

A function is a chunk of composed, reusable code that is utilized to play out one or more related activity. Functions are useful since they give better seclusion to your application and a high level of code reusing.

As you definitely know, Python gives you numerous inherent functions including print(), and so on yet you can likewise make your own particular functions. Such functions are known as user defined functions

How to define a function:

You can create any function that gives the required duty. Here are straightforward principles while creating functions in Python:

- Any function begins with the special words i.e.def this will be followed by the name of your customized function and brackets (( )).
- All of the input parameters must be placed in the parentheses. You can likewise characterize parameters inside these brackets.
- The principal explanation of a capacity can be a discretionary proclamation - the documentation string of the function.
- The code chunk inside each function begins with a colon (:) and is indented.
- The announcement return [expression] exits a capacity, alternatively going back an expression to the guest. An arrival explanation without any contentions is the same as return.
-

Calling a function:

Characterizing a function just gives it a name, determines the parameters that are to be incorporated into the capacity and structures the pieces of code. Once the essential structure of a capacity is settled, you can execute it by calling it from another capacity or specifically from the Python brief.

Function definition

```
def printme( var ):

  "This prints string into this function"

  print var

  return;
```

```
# Function definition

printme("First call")

printme("Second call")
```

Furthermore, following arguments can also be used to call a function:

- Arguments which are keyword
- Arguments which are required
- Arguments which variable-length

Default arguments

Chapter 10-Lists and Dictionaries in Python

List is a holder that holds various different articles, in a given request. This executes the grouping convention, furthermore permits you to include and expel objects from the arrangement.

Making Lists:

To make a list, put various expressions in square sections:

- L = []
- L = [expression, ...]

This develop is called display list. Python likewise underpins registered records, called list perceptions. In its most straightforward structure, a rundown cognizance has the accompanying linguistic structure:

L = [expression for variable in sequence] where the expression is assessed once, for each thing in the succession.

The expressions can be anything; you can put a wide range of items in records, including different records, and numerous references to a solitary article.

The most fundamental information structure in Python is the sequence. Every component of an arrangement is relegated a number its position or record. The principal list is zero; the second list is one, et cetera. Python has six implicit sorts of sequences, yet the most well-known ones are tuples and list, which we would find in this instructional exercise.

There are sure things you can do with all arrangement sorts. These operations incorporate adding, indexing, slicing, multiplying, and checking for membership. What's more, Python has worked in multiple functions for finding the length of a succession and for discovering its biggest and littlest components.

Lists of Python:

The rundown is a most flexible datatype accessible in Python which can be composed as a rundown of comma-isolated qualities (things) between square sections. Vital thing around a rundown is that things in a rundown need not be of the same sort.

Making a rundown is as straightforward as putting diverse comma-isolated qualities between square sections. For instance

- array1 = ['chemistry', 'physics', 2000, 2010];
- array2 = [1, 2, 3, 4, 5];

Expressions:

- Len-> length
- []+[]-> concatenation
- ['A']*4->repetition
- 3in [1,2,3]-> membership

Dictionaries:

Every key is isolated from its quality by a colon (:). The things are isolated by commas, and the entire thing is encased in wavy supports. An unfilled word reference with no things is composed with only two wavy props, this way: {}.

Keys are novel inside a lexicon while qualities may not be. The estimations of a word reference can be of any sort; however the keys must be of an unchanging information sort, for example, strings, numbers, or tuples.

Access Values in Dictionary:

In order to gain access dictionary elements, you can utilize the well-known square sections alongside the way to acquire its worth. Following is an example:

data = {'Name': 'hina', 'Age': 8, 'Class': 'second'}

print "data['Name']: ", data['Name']

print "data['Age']: ", data['Age']; The outcome will be the name and age.

Conclusion

To put in a nutshell, this book provides an insight about the advance programming language, Python. Python is a high-level language which easily understandable. Moreover, it has close proximity with the previous programming languages namely, C, C++ and Java. This book is quite useful for the beginners since it has been designed in such a manner that a beginner programmer can understand the terminologies used in this book. This book discusses multiple aspects of python.

Python is a basic yet critical dialect with such structure that underscores on the clarity. This component reduces the cost of backing of the task. Python, what's more, supports groups and modules, which empowers program measured quality and code reuse. The Python translator and the far reaching standard library are accessible in source or parallel structure without charge for every single significant stage, and can be direct scattered.

A great part of the time, programming engineers succumbed to Python in light of the expanded adequacy it offers. The cycle of change, test and investigate is exceptionally capable and speedy as an aftereffect of the nonattendance of game plan step. Exploring Python endeavors is fundamental: a bug or unpleasant information will neglect to bring around a division issue. On the other hand perhaps, when the mediator finds a mistake, it raises an unprecedented case. Precisely when the assignment doesn't get the extraordinary case, the center individual prints a stack take after.

Firstly, it provides an overview of python. Then, it helps in establishing the environment required for Python's setup in various operating systems. Moreover, the basic syntax of Python is discussed in detail as well. This will facilitate the programmer in developing applications. Further, variable types and basic operators for Python are explained extensively to clarify the ambiguities. Additionally, the procedure undertaken for decision making is also elaborated in here. In addition to that, loops and numbers which are used in Python are described here as well. Adding to this is the extraordinary efficiency of this book, which ensures the clarification of all of the difficulties faced by the beginner.

These features include strings and console outcomes, control flow in Python, the extremely important functions of Python, and lists and dictionaries are also explained in the book. Therefore, all of the aspects that are important in understanding this programming language are added to facilitate the programmers.

Thanks again for taking the time to download this book!

You should now have a good understanding of PYTHON programming, and be able to complete simple tasks.

If you enjoyed this book, please take the time to leave me a review on Amazon. I appreciate your honest feedback, and it really helps me to continue producing high quality books.